Brawl Stars Ultimate Gu Brawler, Strategy, and Dominate the Arena

The Complete Guide to Tips, Tricks, and Strategies for Beginners and Pros Alike

Introduction to Brawl Stars

What is Brawl Stars?

Brawl Stars is a fast-paced, multiplayer online battle arena (MOBA) game developed by Supercell, the creators of other popular games like Clash of Clans and Clash Royale. Launched globally in December 2018, Brawl Stars combines colorful visuals, dynamic gameplay, and unique characters known as "Brawlers." It's available on both iOS and Android platforms.

Why It's One of the Most Popular Mobile Games

Brawl Stars has become one of the most beloved mobile games due to its accessibility, constant updates, and variety of gameplay styles. Its engaging mechanics appeal to both casual players and competitive gamers. Key factors contributing to its popularity include:

- **Diverse Gameplay:** Players can explore various game modes, each offering a unique experience.
- **Regular Updates:** New Brawlers, skins, maps, and events keep the game fresh.
- **Competitive Scene:** A strong esports presence and regular tournaments encourage community engagement.
- **Social Interaction:** Players can team up with friends, join clubs, and communicate during matches.

Overview of the Game's Objectives, Modes, and Appeal

Objectives:

The primary goal in Brawl Stars depends on the selected mode, but generally, players aim to defeat opponents, collect resources, and achieve specific objectives like controlling zones or scoring goals.

Game Modes:

- **Gem Grab:** Teams of three compete to collect and hold 10 gems.
- **Showdown:** A free-for-all or duo battle royale where the last player or team standing wins.
- **Brawl Ball:** A soccer-inspired mode where players score goals using their Brawlers.
- **Heist:** Teams attack or defend a safe filled with treasure.
- **Bounty:** Players earn points by defeating opponents while avoiding being eliminated.
- **Special Events and Seasonal Modes:** Limited-time modes that provide unique challenges and rewards.

Appeal:

Brawl Stars combines approachable mechanics with depth, offering something for everyone. Its vibrant art style and quirky Brawlers draw players in, while strategic gameplay and a competitive ranking system keep them engaged. The blend of teamwork and individual skill ensures a rewarding experience, whether you're playing casually or chasing leaderboard dominance.

1. **Download the Game:**
   - For **iOS users**: Open the App Store, search for "Brawl Stars," and tap *Download.*
   - For **Android users**: Open the Google Play Store, search for "Brawl Stars," and tap *Install.*
2. **Initial Setup:**
   - Once the game is installed, launch it and accept the terms of service.

- o Link your game to a Supercell ID to save progress and play across devices.
- o Complete the quick tutorial to learn the basics of movement, shooting, and using special abilities.

Game Interface Walkthrough

- **Main Screen:**
    - o **Play Button:** Launch a match in the selected game mode.
    - o **Game Mode Selector:** Shows the available modes, including Gem Grab, Showdown, and special events.
    - o **Events Tab:** Displays current and upcoming game modes and their rewards.
- **Trophy Road:** Tracks your progress and unlocks rewards like Brawlers, coins, and power points as you earn trophies.
- **Brawlers Tab:** View, select, and upgrade your Brawlers. Each Brawler has unique stats, abilities, and skins.

- **Shop:** Purchase skins, coins, power points, and Brawl Pass rewards using gems or real money.
- **Club Tab:** Join or create a club to connect with other players and participate in club activities.
- **Settings:** Adjust controls, sound, and graphics. Use this to link your Supercell ID.

Understanding Trophies, Brawlers, and Progression

- **Trophies:**
  - Earned by winning matches in any mode.
  - The more trophies you have, the higher your Trophy Road progress.
  - Losing matches can result in a trophy loss for higher-level players.
- **Brawlers:**
  - Unlock new Brawlers through Trophy Road, Brawl Pass, or loot boxes.
  - Each Brawler has unique abilities:

- **Basic Attack:** Standard offensive move.
- **Super Ability:** A more powerful, game-changing move.
- **Star Powers and Gadgets:** Unlockable upgrades that add strategic depth.
  - Players can upgrade Brawlers using power points and coins to improve their stats.

- **Progression:**
  - Advancing in the Trophy Road unlocks new Brawlers, rewards, and game modes.
  - Completing daily quests and seasonal challenges earns progress in the Brawl Pass.
  - Participate in special events and challenges for additional rewards and bragging rights.

With a solid grasp of these basics, you'll be ready to dive into the fast-paced action of Brawl Stars!

Chapter 1: Mastering the Basics

Controls and Gameplay: Movement, Aiming, and Shooting

- **Movement:**
  - Use the **joystick** on the left side of the screen to move your Brawler around the map.
  - Precise movement is key for dodging enemy attacks and positioning yourself for offense or defense.
- **Aiming and Shooting:**
  - Use the **joystick on the right side** to aim your attacks. Drag it to set the direction, then release to fire.
  - Tap the joystick to automatically attack the nearest target (Auto-Aim). This is quicker but less accurate and less effective in advanced play.
  - Use your **Super Ability** by charging it through attacks. Once charged, a

yellow icon appears. Drag or tap to unleash your Super.

- **Strategic Tips:**
  - Learn to balance Auto-Aim with manual aiming based on the situation. Auto-Aim works well in close range but can miss distant or moving targets.
  - Always keep moving to make yourself harder to hit, especially when reloading.
  - Take advantage of **bushes** for hiding and **walls** for cover.

Game Modes

Gem Grab

- **Objective:**
  - Teams of 3 collect and hold 10 gems from the mine at the center of the map.
  - Hold the gems for 15 seconds to win.

- **Key Strategies:**

  0. **Team Roles:**
     - **Gem Carrier:** Collects and holds gems; stays safe and avoids unnecessary risks.
     - **Support:** Protects the gem carrier and applies pressure on enemies.
     - **Aggressor:** Engages enemies and keeps them away from the gem mine.

  1. **Control the Center:**
     - Gain control of the center area to dominate gem collection.
     - Use cover effectively to contest the mine and retreat when needed.

  2. **Countdown Management:**
     - If the enemy team initiates the countdown, focus on eliminating their gem carrier to reset it.

- **Winning Tip:**
  - Prioritize survival over holding many gems. A well-timed retreat can secure a victory.

Showdown (Solo and Duo)

- **Objective:**
  - Be the last player (Solo) or team (Duo) standing in a shrinking battlefield.
  - Collect **Power Cubes** from crates or fallen opponents to increase your health and damage.
- **Key Strategies:**

  0. **Start Carefully:**
     - Avoid rushing into combat early. Focus on collecting Power Cubes and scouting for enemies.
     - Use bushes to ambush or escape from opponents.
  1. **Monitor the Poison Cloud:**

- The play area shrinks over time. Stay ahead of the poisonous gas while positioning yourself strategically.

2. **In Duo Mode:**
   - Stick with your partner to avoid being outnumbered.
   - If one partner falls, they will respawn after a brief timer if the other survives.

- **Winning Tip:**
  - Patience pays off. Avoid unnecessary risks, especially when low on health. Let stronger opponents weaken each other before making your move.

Mastering the basics of movement, aiming, and understanding these foundational modes will set you up for success as you explore more advanced gameplay in Brawl Stars!

Heist

- **Objective:**
  - Two teams of 3 compete to either **defend** or **attack** a treasure safe.
  - Attackers aim to break into the safe and steal its treasure, while defenders try to protect it.
  - The team that causes the most damage to the enemy's safe wins the match, or if the attacking team manages to destroy it before the time runs out, they win.
- **Key Strategies:**

  0. **Attackers:**
     - Focus on dealing damage to the safe while managing to stay alive.
     - Use long-range Brawlers to avoid taking too much damage from defenders.
     - Coordinate with teammates to focus fire on the safe while keeping enemy Brawlers at bay.

1. **Defenders:**
   - Use crowd control Brawlers to slow or push back the attackers.
   - Prevent attackers from getting close to the safe by controlling key areas of the map.
   - Stay aggressive and try to eliminate attackers before they do too much damage.

- **When to Choose Heist:**
  - Choose Heist if you enjoy **strategic teamwork** and **high-risk gameplay** where both attacking and defending require coordination and precision.

Brawl Ball

- **Objective:**
  - Teams of 3 play a soccer-inspired game, where the goal is to score 2

points by shooting a ball into the opposing team's goal.

- o Players need to both score and defend their goal.

- **Key Strategies:**

  0. **Attackers:**
     - Focus on ball control and positioning to shoot goals.
     - Coordinate passes to keep the ball moving and catch defenders off guard.

  1. **Defenders:**
     - Block the enemy Brawlers from reaching the ball and shoot on your goal.
     - Use knockback or slow abilities to control enemy Brawlers' movements near your goal.

  2. **Support:**
     - Provide backup to both attackers and defenders by controlling the middle of the map and collecting power-ups.

- **When to Choose Brawl Ball:**
  - Choose Brawl Ball if you enjoy **team-based, tactical plays** with a bit of sports flair. It requires both offensive and defensive skills, making it a great choice for players who enjoy well-coordinated, action-packed gameplay.

Hot Zone

- **Objective:**
  - Teams of 3 battle to control specific areas of the map called **Hot Zones**.
  - The team that controls the zone the longest wins the match, with the control time building up over time.
- **Key Strategies:**

  0. **Controlling Zones:**
     - Focus on holding and defending the Hot Zone. Prioritize staying within the

zone, but avoid staying too long in one spot to minimize the risk of enemy ambushes.

1. **Enemy Pressure:**
   - Apply constant pressure to enemies trying to control the zone. Focus on taking down key Brawlers who pose a threat to your team's control.
   - Use ranged Brawlers to take advantage of the wide spaces around the Hot Zone.

2. **Positioning:**
   - Position your team around the Hot Zone to prevent the opposing team from easily capturing it. Hold key chokepoints.

- **When to Choose Hot Zone:**
  - Choose Hot Zone if you like **territory control mechanics** and **strategic positioning**. This mode rewards teamwork and map control, with

intense competition around Hot Zones.

Knockout

- **Objective:**
  - Teams of 3 battle in a knockout-style tournament, where players must eliminate the opposing team.
  - Each team has one chance to win a round, and the match is played in multiple rounds. The team that wins two rounds first wins the match.
- **Key Strategies:**

  0. **Survival is Key:**
     - Knockout is focused on **elimination**, so it's important to avoid taking unnecessary damage and focus on surviving to the next round.
     - When you're ahead, play more cautiously to secure the win

without risking unnecessary deaths.

1. **Team Coordination:**
    - Teamwork is essential in Knockout, as a single player's mistake can cost your team the round. Coordinate with your team to pick off the enemy Brawlers one by one.

2. **Positioning:**
    - Use the map's layout to your advantage, stay aware of safe zones, and work with your teammates to trap and eliminate the enemy team.

- **When to Choose Knockout:**
    - Choose Knockout if you enjoy **elimination-style** matches with a focus on **survival, precision**, and **teamwork**. It's a great mode for players who prefer slower, tactical battles with high stakes.

When and How to Choose Each Mode:

- **Gem Grab:**
  - Choose when you want a fast-paced, team-oriented game with a focus on **collection** and **teamwork**. It's good for players who like to focus on objectives while managing their position.
- **Showdown:**
  - Opt for Solo if you enjoy **survival** and **intense solo competition**. Choose Duo if you prefer a more cooperative style with a teammate, especially if you want to mix strategy and teamwork in a survival setting.
- **Heist:**
  - Select when you want a **tactical, high-stakes mode** involving both offense and defense. It's great for players who enjoy **sieging** and

protecting objectives, requiring precision and coordination.

- **Brawl Ball:**
  - o Ideal when you're in the mood for a more **action-packed, team-based sports challenge.** Choose Brawl Ball for dynamic gameplay and quick goal-scoring, especially if you enjoy both offense and defense.

- **Hot Zone:**
  - o Choose when you want a **territory control** experience that requires **smart positioning** and **map control.** This mode is for players who enjoy controlling key locations and outsmarting opponents.

- **Knockout:**
  - o Pick this mode when you prefer **elimination rounds** and **team survival.** It's ideal for players who like **high-stakes** matches where team coordination is crucial to winning each round.

By understanding each mode's nuances, you can make more informed decisions about which mode best suits your playstyle and goals for the day!

Chapter 2. Unlocking and Upgrading Brawlers

How to Unlock Brawlers:

There are several ways to unlock new Brawlers in **Brawl Stars**. Each method offers a unique approach to collecting characters.

1. **Trophy Road:**
   o As you **earn trophies** by winning matches, you progress along the **Trophy Road**.

- o This unlocks Brawlers at specific trophy milestones (e.g., 10, 100, 500 trophies).
- o Brawlers unlocked through the Trophy Road are typically early-game characters.

2. **Boxes (Brawl Boxes and Big Boxes):**
   - o **Brawl Boxes** and **Big Boxes** contain rewards such as **coins**, **Power Points**, and sometimes **new Brawlers**.
   - o You can earn Brawl Boxes by completing daily quests, events, or purchasing them using in-game currency (gems or coins).
   - o Opening boxes gives you a chance to unlock **rare** or **epic** Brawlers, and upgrading them through Power Points.

3. **Events and Brawl Pass:**
   - o Certain **special events** offer limited-time opportunities to unlock or earn Brawlers.

- **Brawl Pass** is a seasonal feature that provides rewards for completing challenges and leveling up the pass. You can unlock **exclusive Brawlers** or **skins** by progressing through the pass tiers.
- Brawl Pass also rewards **Power Points**, **coins**, and other upgrades.

4. **Shop (Optional Purchase):**
   - Sometimes, new Brawlers can be purchased directly using **gems** or **coins** in the **shop**.
   - These Brawlers are typically offered during special promotions or as part of exclusive packages.

Brawler Classes and Roles:

Brawlers are categorized into different **classes** based on their abilities, playstyle, and role within a team. Each class offers a different tactical advantage, and understanding their roles is key to success.

1. **Damage Dealers (Attackers):**

- o **Role:** Primary damage dealers, focused on eliminating enemies.
- o **Characteristics:** High damage output but usually weaker health.
- o **Examples:**
  - **Shelly**: A shotgun-wielding Brawler with close-range burst damage.
  - **Nita**: A mid-range Brawler with decent damage and a summoning bear to help in combat.
- o **Playstyle Tips:** Focus on attacking enemy Brawlers, staying behind tanks, and using terrain for cover.

2. **Tank:**
   - o **Role:** Absorbs damage and protects teammates.
   - o **Characteristics:** High health and durability, but typically lower damage output.
   - o **Examples:**

- **El Primo**: A powerful tank with strong close-range damage and great mobility.
- **Bull**: A tank with high health and a shotgun for dealing close-range damage.
  - **Playstyle Tips:** Use your durability to initiate fights, push enemies back, and distract opponents for your teammates.

3. **Support:**
   - **Role:** Provides healing, buffs, or other advantages to the team.
   - **Characteristics:** Typically has lower health but important utility abilities.
   - **Examples:**
     - **Pam**: A healer who can drop a healing turret to support allies.
     - **Barley**: A long-range thrower who can control space with area-of-effect damage and debuffs.
   - **Playstyle Tips:** Stay behind your team, use healing or buffs to support

them, and control areas with your unique abilities.

4. **Sniper:**
   - **Role:** Long-range damage dealers who can hit enemies from a distance.
   - **Characteristics:** Low health but excellent range and accuracy, making them great for picking off enemies.
   - **Examples:**
     - **Penny**: A sniper with splash damage from her cannon.
     - **Brock**: A long-range missile launcher with high burst damage.
   - **Playstyle Tips:** Stay at a distance from combat, use cover, and pick off enemies without getting close to danger.

5. **Control (Crowd Control/Disruptors):**
   - **Role:** Prevents enemies from escaping, disrupts enemy strategies, and controls areas.

- o **Characteristics:** Often have abilities that slow, push back, or disorient enemies.
- o **Examples:**
  - **Tara**: A control Brawler who uses her super to pull enemies into a circle, disabling them temporarily.
  - **Colette**: A Brawler who can damage enemies relative to their current health, useful for dissuading aggressive attacks.
- o **Playstyle Tips:** Control the flow of the game by forcing enemies into poor positions and helping your team secure important areas.

6. **Throwers:**
   - o **Role:** Uses projectiles to deal damage over an area or at a distance, often behind cover.
   - o **Characteristics:** Low health and range but powerful splash damage abilities.
   - o **Examples:**

- **Barley**: Throws bottles that explode on impact, dealing area damage.
- **Darryl**: Uses a rolling barrel to escape or attack enemies from unexpected angles.
- **Playstyle Tips:** Use your range and splash damage to control choke points and disrupt enemy formations, while avoiding getting too close to opponents.

Upgrading Brawlers:

Once you unlock a Brawler, you can **upgrade** them to improve their **health, damage**, and **super abilities**.

1. **Power Points:**
   - You earn **Power Points** through boxes, events, or the Brawl Pass.
   - Use **Power Points** to level up your Brawler, making them stronger and

unlocking their **Star Powers** and **Gadgets**.

2. **Coins:**

   ○ Coins are used to upgrade your Brawler's level. The more you level up, the more **Power Points** you need, and the more coins you'll require.

   ○ Coins are earned through victories, quests, and opening boxes.

3. **Star Powers & Gadgets:**

   ○ **Star Powers** are unique abilities that can further customize your Brawler's playstyle.

   ○ **Gadgets** provide one-time-use abilities that offer tactical advantages in combat (e.g., healing, mobility, or damage boosts).

   ○ These are unlocked at higher Brawler levels and can greatly enhance their effectiveness.

By understanding how to unlock and upgrade Brawlers, as well as recognizing their classes and roles, you can build a versatile team that's prepared for any situation in **Brawl Stars**!

Tanks, Damage Dealers, Support, and Hybrids

Tanks

- **Role:** Tanks are the heavy hitters who absorb damage and control the battlefield, providing cover for other Brawlers.
- **Characteristics:** High health, decent damage output, but lower range.
- **Examples:**
  - **El Primo**: A brawler with high health, great mobility, and powerful close-range attacks. His Super allows him to jump onto enemies, disrupting their positions.
  - **Bull**: A tank with a shotgun that deals massive damage up close, complemented by his ability to charge through obstacles and enemies with his Super.

- **Strengths:** Tanks can engage directly, soak up damage, and create opportunities for teammates. They excel at leading the charge and controlling key areas.
- **Weaknesses:** They struggle against ranged enemies and need support to maximize their effectiveness.

Damage Dealers

- **Role:** Damage Dealers are the primary source of offensive power. They focus on dealing high damage to enemies and eliminating threats.
- **Characteristics:** High damage output, but lower health and survivability.
- **Examples:**
    - **Shelly**: A shotgun-wielding brawler who can deal heavy burst damage at close range.
    - **Brock**: A long-range missile launcher that can deal high burst damage from afar, great for picking off enemies at a distance.

- **Strengths:** Damage Dealers shine in aggressive, offensive play. They can melt through enemies quickly when positioned correctly.
- **Weaknesses:** They are vulnerable to tanky Brawlers and need proper positioning to avoid getting eliminated quickly.

Support

- **Role:** Supports provide utilities like healing, buffs, debuffs, or map control. They help teammates stay in the fight longer and control the flow of battle.
- **Characteristics:** Typically have lower health, but powerful utility abilities that assist the team.
- **Examples:**
  - **Pam**: Heals teammates in a large area with her turret, making her invaluable for prolonged fights.
  - **Barley**: Can control zones with area-of-effect damage, creating barriers for

enemy movement and helping his team dominate an area.

- **Strengths:** Supports are crucial for keeping teammates alive and enabling strategic plays, offering a lot of utility.
- **Weaknesses:** They lack offensive firepower and are often vulnerable if left unprotected.

Hybrids (Versatile Brawlers)

- **Role:** Hybrids are Brawlers that can serve multiple purposes, being capable of both dealing damage and providing support or tanking when needed.
- **Characteristics:** Balanced stats that allow them to adapt to a variety of situations.
- **Examples:**
  - **Nita**: She can deal decent damage and summon a bear that helps control areas and provide support.
  - **Gene**: A well-rounded brawler with good damage and the ability to heal or pull enemies towards him using his Super.

- **Strengths:** Hybrids can adapt to changing situations and provide flexible roles, making them reliable in most team compositions.
- **Weaknesses:** Hybrids may not excel as much in one specific role compared to Tanks, Damage Dealers, or Support, but they provide a balanced mix.

Prioritizing Upgrades for Maximum Impact

When upgrading your Brawlers, it's important to consider the following factors for maximizing their effectiveness:

1. **Understand Your Brawler's Role:**
   - **Tanks** should prioritize **health** and **survivability**. Upgrade their **health** and **damage** to make them even more formidable in the frontline. **Gadgets** or **Star Powers** that offer mobility or additional defense are also vital.

- **Damage Dealers** should focus on **damage output**. Upgrading **damage** first will allow them to eliminate enemies quickly. Consider upgrading **Super abilities** that increase their overall burst potential, like Shelly's Super.
- **Supports** benefit from upgrades that enhance their **healing** or **utility**. Maximize their **Super abilities** to improve their healing, buffing, or area control. Upgrading **Power Points** for Star Powers that affect the team's survivability will ensure the best results.
- **Hybrids** need a balanced upgrade path. Prioritize **damage** first for offensive capabilities, then improve **health** or **supporting abilities** to make them adaptable in any situation.

2. **Upgrade Path:**
   - **First Priority:** Always prioritize **damage** for offensive Brawlers

(Damage Dealers) or **health** for defensive Brawlers (Tanks). Brawlers with **area control** (like Barley) should focus on **range** and **control effects**.

  o **Second Priority:** For **Supports**, upgrade **Star Powers** and **Super abilities**. For **Tanks**, focus on **damage** or **additional survivability**.

  o **Third Priority:** For **Hybrids**, upgrade abilities that give them flexibility, such as a combination of **damage**, **health**, and **utility upgrades**.

3. **Star Powers and Gadgets:**

  o **Star Powers** should be upgraded as soon as you unlock them, as they provide extra utility or enhancements to your Brawler's core abilities.

  o **Gadgets** add another layer of strategic depth. Prioritize upgrading **gadgets** that give you control over the battlefield (such as healing, stun, or mobility), depending on your role and playstyle.

4. **Synergy with Your Team:**

- Consider the **team composition** when upgrading. For example, if you are playing with a Tank, upgrading their **health** and **Super** could make them more reliable, whereas **Damage Dealers** should be focused on maximizing their **offensive capabilities**.
- If you play with a **Support Brawler**, their **utility upgrades** should be prioritized to keep the team alive and effective in controlling the match.

5. **Prioritize Upgrades Based on Game Mode:**

- For **Gem Grab**, prioritize Brawlers with **damage** and **survivability** (Tanks, Damage Dealers).
- For **Brawl Ball**, focus on Brawlers with **mobility** and **damage** (Hybrids or Damage Dealers), but also consider Brawlers with utility for **defense** (Support Brawlers with healing).

o For **Showdown**, focus on **damage** and **survivability**, especially if you're solo (Damage Dealers and Tanks).

o For **Hot Zone**, prioritize **area control** and **support** Brawlers (Brawlers with AoE damage or healing abilities).

o For **Heist**, balance between **damage** (to destroy the safe) and **tankiness** (to soak up damage from opponents).

By following these upgrade priorities, you'll maximize your Brawler's potential, adapt to different situations, and ensure your team can shine in various game modes.

Chapter 3. Advanced Strategies for Winning

Map-Specific Strategies

Each map in **Brawl Stars** presents unique opportunities and challenges. Understanding map layouts and how to adapt your strategy to them is key to securing victories. Here's how to optimize your playstyle for different types of maps:

1. **Gem Grab Maps:**
   - **Strategy:**
     - **Control the center**: The middle area usually has gems. Prioritize holding this central

location while managing to fend off enemies trying to grab gems.

- **Positioning and rotation**: Always rotate your position in the middle, moving back to pick up gems and fight off enemies. Avoid getting too greedy by picking up gems in the open without backup.

- **Brawlers with speed or range**: Brawlers with high mobility or range (like **Colt**, **Brock**, or **Mortis**) are ideal, as they can quickly contest the center and eliminate opponents from a distance.

2. **Showdown (Solo/Duo) Maps:**
   o **Solo:**
      - **Survival-focused**: Prioritize **survival** over aggression, especially in Solo Showdown. Use **tanks** like **Bull** or **El Primo** to absorb damage and outlast

opponents, or **damage dealers** like **Brock** to eliminate enemies from a distance.

- **Positioning**: Stick to the outer edges of the map, avoiding early conflict. As the map shrinks, move toward the center and strategically eliminate other players.
- **Use of bushes**: Take advantage of **bushes** for surprise attacks and hiding when necessary.

- **Duo:**
  - **Team coordination**: Work closely with your partner to corner and eliminate enemies. Using a **tank and support** combo works well, as the tank can engage, while the support Brawler heals or offers crowd control (e.g., **Pam** and **El Primo**).
  - **Cover each other's weaknesses**: If one player is a

close-range tank, the other can be a long-range sniper or area controller.

3. **Heist Maps:**
    o **Attackers' Strategy:**
        ▪ **Focus on the safe**: Attackers should always focus on dealing damage to the enemy's safe while also keeping enemies at bay. Long-range Brawlers (e.g., **Brock**, **Penny**) are perfect for attacking the safe from a distance without exposing themselves too much.
        ▪ **Maximize safe damage**: Avoid distraction by enemies. Once you engage the enemy team, always go back to the safe afterward to deal damage.
    o **Defenders' Strategy:**
        ▪ **Disrupt attackers**: Defenders need to disrupt attackers by controlling key areas and using

knockback or stun abilities (e.g., **Tara's** Super, **BB's** stun).

- **Control map space**: Position yourself near the safe but far enough to contest attackers and prevent them from getting free damage. Consider using **bushes** to sneak up on attacking Brawlers.

4. **Brawl Ball Maps:**
   o **Strategy:**
      - **Team play**: Coordinate well with your teammates for passing the ball and taking turns in offense and defense. For example, use **El Primo's** Super to clear the path while your teammate shoots the ball.
      - **Tank-based offense**: A **tank** like **Bull** can bulldoze through enemies to get to the ball, while a **damage dealer** like **Brock** can shoot from the back.

- **Defenders' role**: Use **Support Brawlers** like **Pam** or **Poco** to heal teammates while staying back to protect the goal. Also, consider **stun** or **slow** Brawlers to disrupt the enemy's offense.
- **Brawlers with mobility**: For **offense**, Brawlers like **Mortis** or **Tara** (with their mobility or crowd control) are useful for moving quickly around the map and passing the ball.

5. **Hot Zone Maps:**
   - **Strategy:**
     - **Area control**: Focus on holding the Hot Zone as long as possible, but don't let enemies push you out. Use **ranged Brawlers** or **throwers** (like **Barley** or **Sprout**) to control the center from a distance.
     - **Tank or support combo**: Having a **tank** to disrupt enemies and a **support**

Brawler (like **Pam** or **Byron**) to heal and keep you in the zone is highly effective.

- **Aggression and retreat**: Don't stay in the Hot Zone when heavily outnumbered. If you need to retreat, fall back to an open area to heal and regroup.

6. **Knockout Maps:**
   o **Strategy:**
      - **Elimination is key**: Knockout is all about survival and precision. Focus on taking out the weakest members of the opposing team first and then finish the rest. Use **long-range Brawlers** to pick off enemies or **control Brawlers** like **Tara** to force opponents into difficult situations.
      - **Positioning and map control**: Take advantage of map layout to gain high ground or control choke points. **Tanks** can be

used to engage and disrupt, while **damage dealers** can follow up with quick eliminations.

Team Composition for Synergy

Team composition in **Brawl Stars** is crucial for creating a balanced and effective team. A strong team is built on **synergy**, ensuring that each player's strengths complement the others. Here are some tips for optimizing team composition:

1. **Balanced Roles:**
   - A well-balanced team should consist of **at least one tank**, **one damage dealer**, and **one support Brawler** (or hybrid Brawler).
   - **Tanks** (e.g., **El Primo, Bull**) lead the charge by absorbing damage and pushing the offensive, especially in modes like **Heist** or **Brawl Ball**.

- **Damage Dealers** (e.g., **Brock, Shelly**) should stay behind the tanks to dish out high damage while staying safe from enemy attacks.
- **Support Brawlers** (e.g., **Pam, Poco**) provide healing or buffs to sustain the team and keep them fighting longer. They can also offer crowd control or map manipulation.

2. **Counter-Picking:**
   - Counter-picking is an advanced strategy where you choose Brawlers that directly counter the enemy team. For example:
     - **If the enemy has a tank-heavy composition**, pick **damage dealers** like **Penny** or **Brock** who can deal with tanks from a distance.
     - **If the enemy relies on ranged damage**, use **close-range tanks** like **El Primo** or **Bull** to rush them down and close the gap.

- If the enemy has high **mobility**, choose **stun or crowd control Brawlers** like **Tara** or **Barley** to limit their movement and effectiveness.

3. **Map-Specific Synergy:**
   - On **open maps** like **Brawl Ball** or **Knockout**, prioritize **long-range Brawlers** with mobility and damage (e.g., **Brock, Penny**).
   - For **tighter maps** like **Gem Grab** or **Hot Zone**, focus on **area control Brawlers** and **tanks** (e.g., **Tara, Pam, El Primo**) to contest the zones and protect the objectives.
   - **Duo Showdown** benefits from **tank and damage dealer** combos. A tank like **Bull** paired with a ranged DPS like **Brock** can provide a nice balance of survivability and offense.

4. **Communication and Coordination:**
   - In modes like **Heist** and **Knockout**, communication is key. Use the chat or ping system to coordinate when to

push, retreat, or target specific Brawlers.

- o Working together to control objectives and focus fire on priority targets will often outweigh individual performance.

5. **Flexibility:**

- o Having **flexible Brawlers** (like **Hybrids**) who can play multiple roles allows for smoother adaptation to changing game conditions. For example, **Gene** can serve as a **damage dealer**, but his **Super** can also provide crowd control for better team synergy.

By mastering **map-specific strategies** and focusing on **team composition for synergy**, you'll have the edge in both competitive and casual matches, making it easier to win and climb the ranks in **Brawl Stars**!

Using Gadgets and Star Powers Effectively

Gadgets:

Gadgets are powerful tools that provide temporary abilities to Brawlers, often offering game-changing advantages during matches. Understanding when and how to use them effectively is key to success.

1. **Know Your Gadget's Purpose:**
   - **Healing Gadgets:** Brawlers like **Pam** or **Poco** can use gadgets to heal themselves or their teammates. Use these gadgets during team fights to maintain pressure and outlast opponents.
     - Example: **Pam's** healing turret is crucial in **Gem Grab** and **Hot Zone**, as it provides sustained healing over time to keep your team alive.
   - **Mobility Gadgets:** Gadgets that enhance mobility can help Brawlers like **Mortis** or **Darryl** quickly reposition or escape tight situations.
     - Example: **Darryl's** Roll gadget allows him to dodge incoming

damage and reach enemies or escape after securing a kill.

- o **Control Gadgets:** Some gadgets allow you to control the battlefield or disable enemies (e.g., stuns, slows).
  - Example: **Tara's** gadget can create a stun effect, allowing your team to follow up with heavy attacks, making it a powerful tool in **Knockout** or **Brawl Ball**.
- o **Damage Gadgets:** Many Brawlers have gadgets that deal damage (e.g., **Brock's** rocket or **Barley's** fire bottle).
  - Example: **Brock's** gadget allows him to deal significant damage at range, making it useful for engaging or breaking cover in tight spots.

2. **Timing and Strategic Usage:**
   - o **Don't waste gadgets** early in the game—reserve them for **crucial moments** like engaging in team

fights or securing objectives (e.g., **Heist** safe or **Gem Grab** control).

- o **Use gadgets for escapes**: When you're surrounded or need to break line of sight, using mobility gadgets can give you the chance to **reposition** or **regroup** with your team.

- o **Coordinate gadgets with your team**: Gadgets can be even more effective when used in combination with teammates. For example, **Tara's** Super can pull enemies into a small area, and then **Gene's** gadget can displace them for maximum disruption.

3. **Recharge Time:**

- o Gadgets are not unlimited; they have a cooldown. Understanding the **recharge time** and using them at the optimal moment is crucial. Make sure you don't burn through them too quickly, as they may be needed later in the game when it matters most.

Star Powers:

Star Powers enhance a Brawler's abilities and can significantly influence gameplay. They are unlocked at **Level 9** and can be upgraded to **Level 10**, providing additional power that can swing battles in your favor.

1. **Understand Each Star Power's Strengths:**
   - **Damage Boost:** Some Star Powers increase damage dealt or provide buffs to basic attacks or Super abilities.
     - Example: **Shelly's Shell Shock** Star Power slows down enemies hit by her Super, making them easier to eliminate. This is great for controlling areas in **Gem Grab** or **Brawl Ball**.
   - **Survivability:** Some Star Powers increase a Brawler's health or help them sustain themselves in fights.

- Example: **Nita's Bear with Me** Star Power grants healing to her summoned bear, allowing it to tank damage while also healing.

o **Utility:** Some Star Powers provide extra utility, such as enhanced mobility or area control.

- Example: **Penny's Plastic Barrier** gives her extra protection for her turret, improving her ability to control space during team fights.

o **Mobility:** Some Brawlers' Star Powers enhance their movement speed or help them reposition quickly.

- Example: **El Primo's El Fuego** Star Power makes his Super deal area damage when he lands, giving him more versatility in offensive and defensive situations.

2. **Using Star Powers at the Right Time:**

- **Utilize synergy**: Star Powers work best when used in synergy with your team's abilities. For example, **Poco's Tuning Fork** heals nearby allies when he uses his Super, which is great when paired with tanks or other high-damage teammates.

- **Maximize damage**: If your Star Power increases your Brawler's damage output, use it in **team fights** or when targeting objectives like **Heist** safes or **Hot Zone** areas. Timing it right with other abilities can help you **secure kills** or **break through enemy defenses** faster.

- **Use in clutch moments**: Some Star Powers, like **Tara's Black Portal**, can be game-changers in critical moments when you need to turn the tide of a fight.

Understanding and Countering Common Strategies

Brawl Stars players often employ common strategies that, if left unchecked, can dominate the match. Here's how to recognize and counter these strategies effectively:

1. **Tank-heavy Compositions:**
   - o **Common Strategy:** Teams with multiple Tanks (**Bull**, **El Primo**, etc.) rely on absorbing damage and controlling the map.
   - o **Counter Strategy:** Use **long-range Brawlers** with high damage output (e.g., **Brock**, **Penny**) to deal damage from a safe distance. **Control Brawlers** like **Tara** or **Barley** can disrupt Tanks by controlling the area with their Super or gadgets.
   - o **Tip:** Tanks need support to sustain themselves. By focusing on **disrupting their healing** or **kiting**

them, you can take away their effectiveness.

2. **Healer and Support-heavy Compositions:**
   - **Common Strategy:** Teams with a strong support presence (e.g., **Pam**, **Poco**, **Byron**) aim to keep the team alive and create a sustained push.
   - **Counter Strategy:** Focus on **bursting down** the **healers** early. Take out **Pam's turret** or **Byron's healing** by prioritizing these support characters with **high damage output** (e.g., **Brock**, **Shelly**).
   - **Tip:** Use **stun gadgets** (like **Tara's** or **Sprout's**) to disable key healers and buy time for your team to finish them off.

3. **High Mobility Compositions:**
   - **Common Strategy:** Teams with high mobility Brawlers like **Mortis**, **Leon**, or **Darryl** aim to rush in and quickly outmaneuver the enemy.
   - **Counter Strategy:** Use **crowd control** (e.g., **Tara**, **Penny**) or

slowing effects (e.g., **Shelly's** Super or **Colette's** Star Power) to limit their mobility and prevent them from escaping after attacking.

○ **Tip:** Position your Brawlers in a way that forces mobile enemies to engage on your terms. For instance, **Tara's Super** can trap multiple mobile enemies in a confined space.

4. **Disruption and Control Compositions:**

○ **Common Strategy:** Teams focused on area control and disruption, using Brawlers like **Barley**, **Sprout**, or **Tara**, look to lock down key areas.

○ **Counter Strategy:** Use **tanks** or **brawlers with mobility** to dive into the backlines and **eliminate control Brawlers**. For example, **El Primo** or **Bull** can rush in and disrupt the backline, while **long-range Brawlers** (e.g., **Brock**, **Bibi**) can safely attack from afar.

○ **Tip:** If you're playing a **control Brawler** yourself, be mindful of how much **space** you control, and avoid overextending too far into enemy territory.

5. **Objective-focused Strategies (Gem Grab, Heist, Brawl Ball):**

    o **Common Strategy:** Teams focusing on **objective control** rather than just kills, such as **holding gems** in **Gem Grab**, pushing the ball in **Brawl Ball**, or defending the **Heist** safe.

    o **Counter Strategy:** Focus on **disrupting the objective**. For example, in **Gem Grab**, try to disrupt the gem holder by using **high burst damage** or **crowd control**. In **Brawl Ball**, use **stun gadgets** or **positioning** to block the goal or force a turnover.

    o **Tip:** Timing is key in objective-based maps. Wait for the right moment to strike, ensuring you have enough damage to disrupt the enemy's plan while protecting your team's objectives.

By **effectively using gadgets** and **Star Powers**, along with a solid understanding of **common strategies** and how to counter them, you'll be well-equipped to handle almost any situation in **Brawl Stars** and lead your team to victory!

Chapter 4. Comprehensive Guide to Each Brawler

In **Brawl Stars**, each Brawler has unique abilities, strengths, and playstyles. To excel in the game, it's essential to know the best Brawlers to use in different situations and how they synergize with other Brawlers. This guide will help you choose the right Brawler for each mode and provide insights into effective combos and synergies.

Brawler Overview (Organized by Class and Rarity)

Brawlers are classified by both their role (class) and their rarity. We'll break down the Brawlers into their classes (Tanks, Damage Dealers, Support, Hybrids) and by their rarity (Common, Rare, Epic, Mythic, Legendary).

Tanks

1. **Bull (Common)**
   - **Primary Role:** Tank
   - **Attack:** Bull fires a shotgun blast in a spread pattern.
   - **Super:** Charges through enemies, dealing damage and knocking them back.
   - **Best Modes: Gem Grab**, **Heist**, **Brawl Ball**
   - **Best Maps: Double Trouble**, **Safe Zone**
   - **Synergies:** Great with **Poco** for healing and **Pam** for area control.

Shelly and **Brock** can provide ranged support while Bull tanks damage.

2. **El Primo (Epic)**
   - **Primary Role:** Tank
   - **Attack:** El Primo punches in a close-range area, dealing damage in a wide radius.
   - **Super:** Jumps to a location, dealing damage to enemies upon landing.
   - **Best Modes: Brawl Ball, Gem Grab, Heist**
   - **Best Maps: Brawl Ball, Double Trouble**
   - **Synergies:** Works well with **Pam** for healing and **Poco** for support. **Tara's** Super can help control enemies as El Primo jumps in.

Damage Dealers

1. **Brock (Epic)**
   - **Primary Role:** Damage Dealer

- Attack: Fires long-range rockets that deal heavy damage.
- Super: Fires a barrage of rockets that can deal massive damage to enemy Brawlers and structures.
- **Best Modes: Gem Grab, Heist, Knockout**
- **Best Maps: Hot Zone, Gem Grab**
- Synergies: Works well with **Penny** (for extra turret damage) and **Tara** (for crowd control). **Pam** can provide healing during a siege.

2. **Shelly (Common)**
   - **Primary Role:** Damage Dealer
   - Attack: Fires a shotgun blast at close range, dealing significant damage to multiple enemies.
   - Super: A powerful blast that pushes enemies away and deals damage.
   - **Best Modes: Gem Grab, Brawl Ball, Showdown**
   - **Best Maps: Gem Grab, Showdown** (Solo/Duo)

- **Synergies:** Great with **Bull** (for tanks) and **Tara** (for control). **Poco's** healing can keep Shelly in the fight longer.

3. **Bibi (Epic)**
   - **Primary Role:** Damage Dealer
   - **Attack:** Hits enemies with her bat, dealing damage and knocking them back.
   - **Super:** Slams the bat on the ground, creating a shockwave that pushes enemies away and deals damage.
   - **Best Modes: Brawl Ball, Knockout, Gem Grab**
   - **Best Maps: Brawl Ball, Knockout**
   - **Synergies: El Primo** can initiate a dive, while **Poco** can heal and support. **Tara's** crowd control pairs well with Bibi's offensive plays.

Support

1. **Pam (Rare)**
   - **Primary Role:** Support

- o **Attack:** Fires a wide shot that deals damage to enemies.
- o **Super:** Deploys a healing turret that heals nearby allies.
- o **Best Modes: Gem Grab, Hot Zone, Brawl Ball**
- o **Best Maps: Gem Grab, Hot Zone**
- o **Synergies:** Works well with **Bull** and **El Primo** for tanking. **Brock** or **Tara** can deal damage while Pam supports them with healing.

2. **Poco (Rare)**
   - o **Primary Role:** Support
   - o **Attack:** Fires musical notes that heal teammates in their path.
   - o **Super:** A healing blast that heals all nearby teammates.
   - o **Best Modes: Gem Grab, Brawl Ball, Heist**
   - o **Best Maps: Brawl Ball, Gem Grab**
   - o **Synergies:** Pairs well with **Bull** or **El Primo** for tanking. **Poco's** healing is ideal for **Brawl Ball** pushes with tanks.

3. **Byron (Mythic)**

   o **Primary Role:** Support

   o **Attack:** Fires a dart that heals teammates or damages enemies.

   o **Super:** Throws a healing or damaging dart over a long distance.

   o **Best Modes: Gem Grab, Knockout, Heist**

   o **Best Maps: Gem Grab, Hot Zone**

   o **Synergies: El Primo** or **Bull** can tank while **Byron** provides consistent healing. **Tara** and **Tara's** crowd control benefit from **Byron's** support.

Hybrids

1. **Tara (Epic)**

   o **Primary Role:** Hybrid (Damage/Control)

   o **Attack:** Fires a set of cards that deal damage in a spread.

- Super: Creates a vortex that pulls enemies toward her and damages them.
- **Best Modes: Gem Grab, Knockout, Hot Zone**
- **Best Maps: Gem Grab, Knockout**
- **Synergies: Bull** or **El Primo** can capitalize on Tara's **Super**, allowing them to close the distance and secure kills. **Brock** can provide ranged support.

2. **Gene (Mythic)**
   - **Primary Role:** Hybrid (Control/Damage)
   - **Attack:** Fires a magic projectile that damages and pulls enemies toward him.
   - **Super:** Launches a powerful hand that pulls enemies to him and disables them temporarily.
   - **Best Modes: Gem Grab, Knockout, Heist**
   - **Best Maps: Gem Grab, Hot Zone**

- Synergies: **Bull** or **El Primo** can dive in after Gene's **Super** pulls enemies. **Pam** can heal the team while they focus on damage.

Best Maps and Modes for Each Brawler

- **Shelly** excels in close-range combat and is ideal for **Gem Grab** and **Showdown**. Her **Super** can push enemies away, making her effective in **Brawl Ball** and **Heist**.

- **El Primo** dominates **Brawl Ball** and **Gem Grab**, especially when used in the center of the map to absorb damage and push opponents.

- **Poco** and **Pam** are essential support heroes for **Gem Grab** and **Hot Zone** maps, where healing and area control are crucial.

- **Tara** and **Brock** shine in **Gem Grab**, **Knockout**, and **Heist**, where crowd control and damage are the keys to victory.

Combos and Synergies

1. **Bull + Poco/Pam**
   - **Bull** charges in with massive health, while **Poco** or **Pam** keeps him healed, making him nearly unstoppable. This combo is strong in **Gem Grab**, **Brawl Ball**, and **Heist**.

2. **Tara + Gene**
   - **Tara's** Super pulls enemies together, while **Gene's** Super pulls them closer for easy elimination. This combo works well in **Knockout**, **Gem Grab**, and **Brawl Ball**.

3. **El Primo + Shelly**
   - **El Primo** tanks the damage and provides space for **Shelly** to deal massive damage from close range. This duo excels in **Brawl Ball** and **Heist**.

4. **Bibi + Pam/Poco**
   - **Bibi** can push enemies back with her **Super**, while **Pam** or **Poco** heal the

team and provide area control. Great for **Knockout** and **Gem Grab**.

5. **Brock + Penny**

   o **Brock's** long-range damage can destroy enemy cover, while **Penny's** turret controls area and adds more damage. This combo shines in **Gem Grab**, **Heist**, and **Knockout**.

Mastering each Brawler's strengths and understanding synergies is crucial to your success in **Brawl Stars**. By tailoring your team to the mode and map, you can increase your chances of victory and climb the ranks!

Chapter 5. Playing with Friends and Teams

Playing **Brawl Stars** with friends and being part of a team can elevate your gameplay experience. Effective communication, coordination, and teamwork are crucial for dominating matches and climbing the ranks. This section provides tips for collaborating with teammates, creating or joining a **successful club**, and building a strong **team dynamic**.

Importance of Communication and Coordination

1. **Effective Communication:**
   - **Voice Chat:** If you're playing with friends, using voice chat or an external messaging app (like Discord) can significantly improve your communication. Inform your teammates about enemy locations, when to use Supers, or when to retreat.
   - **Ping System:** In **Brawl Stars**, use the in-game ping system to highlight specific areas, enemies, or objectives. Pings help to direct your team's focus without requiring voice communication, which is especially useful in non-voice settings.
   - **Callouts:** Develop a set of common callouts with your team to indicate critical moments:
     - **"Push"**: When the team should advance or attack.

- **"Defend"**: When you need to fall back and protect the objective.
- **"Retreat"**: If the team is overextended and needs to regroup.
- **"All-in"**: When everyone goes for a coordinated push, especially in **Brawl Ball** or **Gem Grab**.

2. **Coordination During Key Moments:**
   - **Objective Control:** In **Gem Grab**, **Hot Zone**, or **Heist**, decide who will focus on the objective while others provide protection or pressure. For example, **Tara's** Super can pull enemies together for a coordinated team push.
   - **Engage and Disengage Together:** Don't go solo in key moments. For example, in **Heist**, if you're attacking, have one or two teammates draw attention while the others focus on the safe.

- **Super Combos:** Some Brawlers work best when their Supers are used in combination. For example, **Tara's** Super can pull enemies in, allowing **El Primo** to dive in and use his Super for maximum damage. Always communicate timing for such plays.

Tips for Creating or Joining a Successful Club

1. **Join a Club with Active Players:**
   - Look for clubs that have active members who play regularly. This will increase your chances of finding teammates for **Club Events** and **Wars**. Check if the club has a strong focus on **competitive play** or casual fun based on your preference.
   - **Club Requirements:** Clubs often have requirements like a certain **trophy count** or level. Choose a club

that aligns with your play style, whether it's focused on casual fun or **competitive progress**.

- ○ **Club Leadership:** A good club is run by a responsible leader who coordinates team efforts, organizes **Club Events**, and fosters a positive environment. Look for clubs with clear leadership and respectful members.

2. **Club Events and Wars:**

- ○ Participate in **Club Wars** to earn rewards and level up your club. Club Wars can also be a great way to test your team's coordination in a competitive environment.

- ○ **Club Events** are also a fun way to participate in regular activities with your teammates. These events provide both rewards and opportunities to experiment with different Brawlers and strategies.

3. **Club Roles:**

- Some clubs organize their members by roles (e.g., tanks, damage dealers, or supports). If you're in a competitive club, make sure you're well-versed in your role, as this can help improve team synergy during **Club Wars** and **events**.
- In casual clubs, members may be more flexible, but it's still important to respect each other's roles and ensure that you have a well-balanced lineup for specific modes.

Building a Strong Team Dynamic

1. **Choose Roles Based on Strengths:**
   - **Tank Role:** If you're good at absorbing damage and engaging enemies, take on the tank role. Brawlers like **Bull**, **El Primo**, and **Frank** excel in this role.
   - **Damage Dealer Role:** If you're more focused on dishing out damage from

a distance, consider Brawlers like **Brock**, **Bibi**, and **Shelly**. They work well when paired with tanks to secure kills.

- o **Support Role:** If you're skilled at keeping teammates alive or controlling the battlefield, play a support role. Brawlers like **Poco**, **Pam**, and **Byron** can heal and provide area control to assist your team.

2. **Team Composition for Synergy:**
   - o A balanced team is key to success. A mix of **tanks**, **damage dealers**, and **supports** ensures your team has the tools to handle different situations. For example:
     - In **Gem Grab**, having a tank (e.g., **Bull**) to hold the center, a damage dealer (e.g., **Brock**) for range, and a support (e.g., **Pam**) to heal can be very effective.

- In **Brawl Ball**, use a **tank** like **El Primo** to contest the ball while a **damage dealer** like **Bibi** or **Shelly** helps score, and a **support** like **Poco** heals.
    - If your team doesn't have a specific role covered, it can lead to problems. Make sure to adjust based on the mode and the Brawlers your team prefers.

3. **Adapt to Opponents and Modes:**
    - Different modes require different strategies and team compositions. For example, **Heist** requires Brawlers that can either push through enemies or defend the safe, so having **damage dealers** like **Brock** or **Tara** is important, along with a **tank** like **Bull** to defend the safe.
    - **Knockout** is a mode focused on eliminating the enemy team, so having a mix of **crowd control** (e.g., **Tara**'s Super) and **damage dealers** is key.

- **Showdown** (Solo or Duo) is another mode where you may not always play with a team, so having versatile Brawlers that can handle different situations (e.g., **Leon**, **Shelly**) will help you adapt.

4. **Don't Overcommit to a Single Strategy:**
   - In team play, flexibility is important. While **Gem Grab** might require a tank in the middle, if you're getting overwhelmed by enemy control Brawlers, you might need to adapt by switching to long-range Brawlers like **Brock** or **Penny** to counter their strategy.

5. **Support Each Other:**
   - **Stay close to teammates:** Whether it's **Gem Grab**, **Heist**, or **Brawl Ball**, positioning close to teammates allows for quick support and counters against enemies who attempt to flank or rush in.
   - **Cover each other's weaknesses:** If you're playing a support role, always

keep an eye on your teammates' health. If you're a damage dealer, ensure that you're not overextended without backup.

Building Team Morale and Fun

1. **Stay Positive:** Teamwork is about keeping the mood upbeat, even when things don't go as planned. Celebrate small victories and learn from mistakes to improve.

2. **Respect and Communication:** Always encourage good sportsmanship. If a teammate makes a mistake, offer constructive advice instead of criticism.

3. **Participate in Fun Activities:** Many clubs organize **Friendly Battles**, **Club Tournaments**, or just play for fun to help members bond and build a stronger team dynamic.

Conclusion:

Playing with friends and in a team is one of the best ways to enjoy **Brawl Stars**. Effective **communication, coordination,** and a **well-balanced team composition** will take your gameplay to the next level. Whether you're in a **Club** working towards **Club Wars** or simply enjoying **Friendly Battles,** having fun and supporting each other is key to success. Keep practicing and building those team bonds for a stronger and more enjoyable experience!

Chapter 6. Climbing the Ladder: Competitive Play

Climbing the ladder in **Brawl Stars** is an exciting challenge that requires strategy, skill, and consistency. Whether you're aiming for **Trophy Road milestones** or competing in ranked matches and tournaments, this section will guide you on how to efficiently gain trophies, prepare for competitive play, and participate in tournaments and events.

How to Gain Trophies Efficiently

1. **Focus on a Few Key Brawlers:**

   o **Master 2-3 Brawlers**: Instead of trying to push every Brawler to high trophies, focus on mastering 2-3 Brawlers that you enjoy and perform well with. This allows you to build consistency in your gameplay and optimize your chances of winning.

   o **Choose Brawlers for Efficiency**: Brawlers with high **survivability** and **damage output** are often the best choices for trophy pushing. For example, **Shelly**, **Brock**, **Penny**, and **Bull** are solid picks for pushing trophies in most modes.

   o **Upgrade Key Brawlers**: Make sure you focus on upgrading Brawlers that are currently strong in the meta, as they will give you a better chance of winning in ranked matches. Prioritize

damage-dealing and **tank Brawlers** that are effective across a variety of modes.

2. **Choose the Right Game Mode:**
   - **Gem Grab** and **Showdown** are often the most efficient modes for trophy pushing. In **Gem Grab**, teamwork is essential, while **Showdown** allows you to control your own fate in solo or duo formats.
   - **Solo Showdown** is ideal for individual performance and can allow skilled players to rack up trophies faster than relying on teams.
   - **Avoid Frustrating Modes**: Some modes, like **Heist**, can be difficult for trophy pushing if your team is uncoordinated, especially in higher trophy ranges. Choose modes where you're most comfortable and confident in your abilities.

3. **Play Smart, Not Just Fast:**
   - **Play Carefully in High Trophy Range**: Once you pass 400-500

trophies with a Brawler, climbing becomes progressively harder. Pay attention to your positioning, avoid rushing in recklessly, and always consider the map and mode you're playing on.

- o **Know When to Stop Pushing**: If you're on a losing streak or facing opponents with significantly higher trophies, it might be wise to pause and avoid further losses. **Trophy Dropping** can be used strategically by players to reset trophies and avoid demotion in highly competitive environments.

4. **Join a Club for Support:**
   - o Playing with clubmates can provide consistent wins and a stronger team synergy, which is important for efficient trophy pushing. Playing with friends or trusted teammates can ensure that you have communication and coordination, which can be a game-changer.

- Participating in **Club Events** and **Club Wars** can also help you earn rewards that assist in upgrading your Brawlers, making trophy pushing easier.

5. **Play During Brawl Pass Seasons:**
   - Take advantage of **Brawl Pass** rewards, which provide bonus trophies, skins, and other rewards as you level up through the pass. Completing the Brawl Pass objectives and milestones will make pushing trophies more efficient and rewarding.

Preparing for Ranked Matches

1. **Know the Meta and Map Rotation:**
   - **Ranked matches** in **Brawl Stars** are influenced by the current meta, which is a combination of the most powerful and balanced Brawlers, as well as the best strategies for each

mode. Stay updated with the **meta** to make the best choices for your trophy pushing.

- o **Map Rotation**: Each season, the map pool changes for different modes. Familiarize yourself with the current map rotation to adjust your strategies accordingly. Certain Brawlers perform better on specific maps due to their attack range, mobility, or ability to control certain areas.

2. **Optimize Your Brawler's Strengths:**

- o **Adapt Brawler Choices for Maps**: For example, **Brock** and **Penny** excel on maps with long sightlines, while **Bull** or **El Primo** are better for close-quarters combat maps like **Brawl Ball** and **Gem Grab**.
- o **Balance Your Team Composition**: If you're playing in a team, make sure to have a good balance between tanks, damage dealers, and supports. For instance, in **Gem Grab**, you want a **tank** to control the center, a

damage dealer to apply pressure, and a **support** to keep teammates alive.

3. **Stay Calm and Focused in Ranked Matches:**

   o **Don't Panic**: Ranked matches can sometimes be high-stress, especially as you push towards **Legendary** trophies. Keep your composure, stay focused on objectives, and avoid unnecessary risks that could lead to an early defeat.

   o **Adapt to the Enemy**: If you find that you're losing to a particular team composition or Brawler, be flexible and adjust your strategy or switch to a different Brawler that counters your opponents. Counter-picking is a big part of **competitive play**.

4. **Understanding Trophies and Ranked Progression:**

   o **Trophy Range**: As you progress, the difficulty of ranked matches increases, and you'll face players with stronger Brawlers. Keep in mind that if you hit a high trophy threshold and start losing consistently, you might have to backtrack a bit, but that's part of the climb.

- **Trophy Road**: The **Trophy Road** provides rewards at various trophy milestones. Be sure to check it regularly, as it provides bonuses such as new Brawlers, skins, and other perks to help with your progression.

Participating in Tournaments and Events

1. **In-Game Events:**
   - **Special Events**: Regular events in **Brawl Stars**, such as **Power Play**, **Brawl Ball Showdowns**, or **Ladder Events**, provide opportunities for players to compete for trophies, exclusive skins, and in-game rewards. Participate in these events

to earn extra trophies or rewards, which will boost your competitive standing.

- o **Event-Specific Strategies**: Each event often requires different strategies. **Brawl Ball** requires teamwork and fast thinking, while **Knockout** is about precision and timing. Understand the rules and dynamics of each event and adapt accordingly.

2. **Tournaments:**
   - o **Competitive Tournaments**: Many **official Brawl Stars tournaments** and **community-organized competitions** exist where you can face off against top-tier players. These tournaments often feature **prize pools**, **exclusive rewards**, and the prestige of being among the best players in the game.
   - o **Preparation for Tournaments**: Practice with your team or individually before entering

tournaments. Ensure that everyone knows their role and has a good understanding of the maps and modes that will be featured.

- o **Register for Events**: Keep an eye on **official social media channels** or **community platforms** for tournament announcements. Some tournaments are open to everyone, while others may require qualifying rounds or club affiliation.

3. **Use Tournament Mode for Practice:**

- o **Scrims** (Practice Matches) in the **Tournament Mode** allow you to refine your skills before facing competitive opponents. Use these to test out new strategies, counter-picks, and practice with your teammates in a controlled setting.

- o **Play with a Set Strategy**: In tournaments, having a game plan for each match is crucial. Communicate with your team about which Brawlers you'll be using, what your objectives are, and how to respond to the enemy's strategies.

4. **Streaming and Watching Competitions:**
   ○ Watching competitive **Brawl Stars** tournaments can help you learn new strategies and see how top players approach different maps and modes. It's a great way to stay updated on the best practices and develop your understanding of the game at a competitive level.

Conclusion:

Climbing the ladder in **Brawl Stars** requires more than just playing the game — it's about **efficient trophy pushing**, **smart strategies** in ranked matches, and **active participation** in tournaments and events. Focus on mastering key Brawlers, optimizing your team composition, and staying informed on the latest game updates to succeed. Whether you're aiming for high trophies, trying to win tournaments, or just enjoying the competitive scene, consistently improving and adapting will ensure you stay on top.

Chapter 7. Mastering Brawl Stars Economy

Brawl Stars has a detailed in-game economy involving **coins**, **power points**, **gems**, and various other resources. Understanding how to earn and spend these resources efficiently is key to progression. This section will guide you through the best ways to earn resources, when to spend or save them, and tips for maximizing rewards from events and offers.

How to Earn Coins, Power Points, and Gems

1. **Coins:**

   - **Daily and Weekly Rewards**: Log in daily to collect your **daily rewards**, which often include coins. Additionally, complete your **Weekly Challenges** to get bonus coins.

   - **Brawl Pass**: As you progress through the **Brawl Pass**, you'll earn coins as rewards, especially as you complete tiers. Don't forget to claim your coin rewards when you level up the pass.

   - **Trophy Road**: Coins are awarded as you progress through the **Trophy Road**. Reaching milestones rewards you with various prizes, including coins.

   - **Events and Game Modes**: Participating in events, such as **Brawl Ball** or **Gem Grab**, can net you coin rewards. Events like **Power Play** also offer coins depending on your performance.

   - **Boxes**: Opening **Brawl Boxes**, **Big Boxes**, or **Mega Boxes** rewards you with coins, as well as **Power Points** and **Gems**. This is often the best way to accumulate a large number of coins early on.

2. **Power Points:**

   o **Chests and Boxes**: Opening any type of box (Brawl, Big, or Mega) will give you **Power Points** for Brawlers you haven't maxed out yet. This is one of the primary ways to level up Brawlers.

   o **Brawl Pass**: Power Points are frequently earned through the **Brawl Pass**, making it a solid way to progress your Brawlers to higher levels.

   o **Trophy Road and Club Rewards**: As you hit specific milestones on the **Trophy Road** or complete **Club Events**, you'll receive Power Points for various Brawlers.

   o **Winning Matches**: In modes like **Showdown**, **Gem Grab**, and **Heist**, you'll also receive Power Points as rewards for winning or completing objectives.

3. **Gems:**

   o **Brawl Pass**: The **Brawl Pass** is a key way to earn **gems**. By progressing through the pass, you receive gems in addition to other rewards like coins and skins.

   o **Daily Offers**: Check the **Shop** for daily offers that might include gem packs for a discounted price. Keep an eye out for special sales.

   o **Opening Boxes**: Occasionally, when opening **Mega Boxes**, you might find **gems** as part of the rewards.

   o **Achievements**: Certain in-game achievements and milestones reward you with gems for completing specific tasks or reaching certain levels.

   o **Events and Tournaments**: Participating in events and tournaments can reward you with gems, so always stay on top of current event calendars to maximize your rewards.

When to Spend vs. Save Resources

1. **Coins:**
   - **Spend on Upgrades**: **Coins** are used to upgrade Brawlers to higher **Power Levels**. Focus on upgrading your favorite or most powerful Brawlers to maximize your performance.
   - **Saving for New Brawlers**: If you're anticipating the release of a new Brawler, it's wise to save some coins for when you unlock that Brawler. This helps you level them up faster and get them into your roster more effectively.
   - **Avoid Over-Spending Early**: Don't rush to upgrade every Brawler you get. Save coins for **higher-tier Brawlers** or those that perform better in competitive modes.

2. **Power Points:**

   - **Focus on Your Main Brawlers**: Don't spread your Power Points too thin. Instead, concentrate on leveling up the Brawlers you enjoy playing the most or those that perform well in the current meta.

   - **Avoid Power Point Overload on Lower-Level Brawlers**: Don't waste Power Points on Brawlers you don't use often or lower-tier Brawlers that you won't invest much time in.

   - **Wait for New Brawlers**: If a new Brawler is about to be released and you are close to unlocking it, it's often better to save your Power Points and use them on the new Brawler to level them up faster.

3. **Gems:**

   - **Brawl Pass**: If you're serious about progressing and unlocking cosmetics, skins, and other rewards quickly, buying the **Brawl Pass** with gems is highly recommended. It provides excellent value for your investment.

- o **Event Offers**: Save gems for special in-game offers or deals that could provide you with value (e.g., **discounted Mega Boxes**, exclusive skins, etc.). Don't waste gems on offers that don't offer good value.

- o **Avoid Over-Spending**: Don't spend gems impulsively on things like **boxes** unless you are sure it's the best way to use them. Gems are a more valuable resource and should be spent wisely.

Tips for Maximizing Rewards from Events and Offers

1. **Maximize Brawl Pass Value:**
   - o **Complete Daily and Weekly Missions**: Focus on completing daily and weekly missions to maximize the rewards from your **Brawl Pass**. Each

tier you unlock gives you rewards like coins, Power Points, and gems.

- o **Claim All Rewards**: Don't miss out on collecting your rewards when you level up the pass, as it often includes valuable resources like coins, Power Points, and gems. The **Brawl Pass** can be an efficient way to stack up resources over time.

2. **Event Bonuses:**

- o **Event-Specific Rewards**: During events, certain modes or challenges offer **double rewards** for wins. Always play these events to maximize coin and Power Point earnings.

- o **Seasonal Events**: Participate in special seasonal events that reward you with extra rewards like **gems**, **coins**, or **exclusive skins**. Keep an eye on the **news** section for upcoming events.

- o **Play During High-Trophy Boosts**: Some events or modes offer **trophy boosts**, which can help you climb faster and earn extra rewards, like gems or coins, for progressing.

3. **Take Advantage of Offers in the Shop:**

   o **Limited-Time Offers**: Occasionally, **Brawl Stars** offers limited-time bundles that provide great value, such as **gems**, **boxes**, or **exclusive skins**. Only spend gems on these offers if you feel it's worth the value.

   o **Special Offers**: When a new Brawler is released or a special event is happening, the in-game shop often features discounts or unique packs that include both **gems** and other resources. Look for these offers and take advantage of them when you can.

4. **Unlock Free Rewards Through Daily Login:**

   o **Daily Login Rewards**: Log in every day to earn **free coins**, **Power Points**, or sometimes even **gems**. These daily bonuses can be a good way to slowly accumulate resources without spending any money.

- o **Events for Free Resources**: Some events offer **free resources** just by participating, so be sure to join them even if you're not looking to actively compete. This way, you can stack up resources while enjoying the game.

5. **Optimize Resource Management in the Shop:**

- o **Mega Boxes and Big Boxes**: Sometimes, the **Mega Box** offers better value in terms of Power Points and Brawler progression than purchasing single **Brawl Boxes**. Keep an eye on special sales and offers to buy boxes when you'll get the most value out of them.

- o **Avoid Over-Spending**: It's easy to get tempted to buy everything, but if you have enough resources for a **Mega Box** or **Brawl Pass**, hold off on buying smaller packages unless they have a limited-time deal attached.

Conclusion:

Mastering the **Brawl Stars** economy is key to progression. Be strategic about **earning** and **spending** coins, Power Points, and gems. Focus on **saving** resources for major milestones, like **Brawl Passes** or event-related rewards, and use them to **maximize** your growth. Participate in as many **events** and **special offers** as possible to increase your rewards without wasting resources. By managing your resources wisely, you'll be able to unlock more content, upgrade your Brawlers faster, and enjoy the game's full potential!

Chapter 8. Staying Ahead with Updates

Brawl Stars is constantly evolving with frequent updates that introduce new **Brawlers**, **modes**, **maps**, and gameplay changes. Staying ahead of these updates is crucial to maintaining an edge in competitive play and ensuring that you always have a strong understanding of the current meta. This section will guide you on how to adapt to new content, utilize patch notes effectively, and stay informed through the **Brawl Stars** community.

How to Adapt to New Brawlers, Modes, and Changes

1. **Master New Brawlers Quickly:**
   - **Unlocking New Brawlers**: Every new update may introduce a new Brawler. Once you unlock a new Brawler, it's important to learn their **abilities**, **stats**, and **best use cases** as quickly as possible.
   - **Experiment with New Brawlers**: Test out the new Brawler in different modes and maps to understand their strengths and weaknesses. Try both **Solo** and **Duo Showdown**, as well as modes like **Gem Grab** and **Brawl Ball**, to see how the Brawler performs in different scenarios.
   - **Look for Synergies**: Some new Brawlers may have synergies with existing Brawlers. For example, a Brawler with a **crowd control** ability might pair well with a **damage dealer**. Experiment with team

compositions and identify which Brawlers work best together.

2. **Adapt to New Modes:**

   o **Learn the Rules of New Modes**: When a new mode is introduced, make sure you understand the core mechanics and objectives of the mode. **Brawl Stars** typically includes a detailed description of the mode, as well as tips on how to perform well in it.

   o **Adjust Your Strategy**: New modes may require a shift in your gameplay style. For example, a mode like **Heist** may require more defensive play, while **Brawl Ball** focuses more on teamwork and precise coordination.

   o **Practice in Limited-Time Modes**: If a limited-time mode is introduced, spend time learning the new mechanics and rules. Some of these modes can have significant rewards, so practicing will help you maximize your chances of success.

3. **Adapt to Gameplay Changes and Balances:**

   o **Understand Balance Changes**: When new **balance changes** (buffs and nerfs) are introduced, it's important to stay informed and adjust your Brawler choices accordingly. A previously weak Brawler may become stronger, while a dominant Brawler might get nerfed.

   o **Test Out the Changes**: After a patch, test out the newly adjusted Brawlers in practice or real matches to gauge the effectiveness of the changes. This will help you quickly identify which Brawlers are now stronger or weaker, and adjust your strategy accordingly.

4. **Use the Training Grounds and Custom Games:**

   o **Practice New Brawlers**: Use the **Training Grounds** to familiarize yourself with new Brawlers and practice their abilities before jumping into actual matches.

- ○ **Custom Games**: When new modes or Brawlers are introduced, playing **Custom Games** with friends can help you experiment and strategize without the pressure of ranked play. These games allow you to understand the nuances of new mechanics.

Utilizing Patch Notes and Meta Analysis

1. **Reading Patch Notes**:
   - ○ **Stay Updated on Patch Notes**: Every time there's a new update or balance change, **Supercell** releases **patch notes**. These notes provide detailed information about new Brawlers, changes to existing ones, adjustments to game mechanics, and bug fixes.
   - ○ **Key Focus Areas**: When reading patch notes, pay special attention to:
     - ▪ **Brawler Changes**: Understand which Brawlers were buffed or

nerfed, as this directly impacts your strategy and team composition.

- **Mode Changes**: Look for any updates to **game modes**, whether it's a new mode or changes to existing ones.

- **Bug Fixes and Tweaks**: Sometimes, fixes or improvements are made to the game's performance or mechanics. Keep track of these as they can impact gameplay.

o **Patch Notes Sources**: Patch notes are available in the **in-game news section**, as well as on official **Brawl Stars** social media platforms and websites.

2. **Meta Analysis**:

o **Analyze the Meta**: After each update, the **meta** (most effective tactics available) often shifts. Some Brawlers become stronger, while others fall out of favor. Pay attention to how these shifts impact team compositions and playstyles.

- **Adapt to the Meta**: If a **tank Brawler** like **Bull** gets a buff, it may be more advantageous to run a tank-heavy team. Conversely, if a **damage dealer** like **Brock** gets a nerf, you may want to pivot to another Brawler who can fill that role more effectively.
- **Watch Competitive Gameplay**: Following top players or competitive **Brawl Stars** tournaments can help you understand how the meta is evolving and what strategies are working for high-level players.

3. **Test New Strategies**:
   - **Experiment with the Meta**: Once you have a general understanding of the meta, don't be afraid to experiment with new strategies. Try out different Brawler combinations, map rotations, and playstyles to find what works best for you in the current environment.

- Adjust to Opponent's Strategy: The meta isn't just about your own team composition; you also need to anticipate and counter your opponent's strategies. If the enemy team is heavily reliant on a particular Brawler, think of ways to counter them (e.g., choosing a Brawler with high mobility to dodge shots).

Staying Informed Through the Brawl Stars Community

1. **Follow Official Channels:**
   - **Brawl Stars Twitter and Instagram**: Supercell frequently posts updates, patch notes, and community highlights on their official social media accounts. These platforms are great for staying up-to-date on the latest news.
   - **Brawl Stars YouTube Channel**: The official **Brawl Stars YouTube**

channel is a great place to watch **developer diaries**, **update videos**, and **event showcases** that provide valuable insights into upcoming changes.

- o **In-Game News Section**: The in-game news section is where you'll find official announcements, events, and details about ongoing and upcoming changes to the game.

2. **Join the Brawl Stars Community:**

- o **Reddit**: The **Brawl Stars subreddit** is a vibrant community where players discuss the latest updates, strategies, and share tips. It's also a great place to ask for advice on new Brawlers or modes.

- o **Discord**: Joining **Brawl Stars** Discord servers can provide real-time discussions, live feedback, and strategies from other players. Many communities also share competitive tips and have dedicated channels for different Brawlers and modes.

o **Brawl Stars Forums**: Engage with other players on official or fan-created forums to exchange knowledge about **new updates** and **patch changes**. This is a great space for both beginners and advanced players to learn from each other.

3. **Watch Content Creators and Streamers:**

   o **YouTube and Twitch**: Many content creators and streamers regularly post updates, gameplay guides, and meta analyses. They often test new Brawlers, modes, and strategies and provide detailed insights that you can apply in your own gameplay.

   o **Community Guides**: Several creators and players share detailed guides on **meta shifts**, **best Brawler combos**, and **strategy changes** after every update. Watching or reading these guides can give you a competitive advantage and help you stay ahead of the curve.

4. **Participate in Community Events**:

○ **Fan Art, Challenges, and Tournaments**: The Brawl Stars community often hosts fan art contests, gameplay challenges, and tournaments. Participating in these events not only helps you stay engaged but also provides an opportunity to learn from other players and showcase your skills.

Conclusion:

Staying ahead with updates in **Brawl Stars** requires proactive engagement with patch notes, meta shifts, and the **Brawl Stars** community. By **adapting** to new Brawlers, modes, and balance changes, as well as utilizing **meta analysis** and community resources, you can always stay on top of the game. Whether you're adjusting to new mechanics, experimenting with strategies, or learning from the community, continuous adaptation is key to maintaining your competitive edge. Stay informed, stay engaged, and you'll be ready to conquer whatever updates come your way!

Chapter 9. Bonus Content

In this section, we'll explore **Brawler Tier Lists**, **Cheat Sheets** for quick references, and **Pro Tips** shared by top players and streamers. These will help you stay at the top of your game, adapt to the ever-changing meta, and improve your overall performance in **Brawl Stars**.

Brawler Tier List: Updated for Current Meta

Brawler **tier lists** are an excellent way to assess which Brawlers are currently the strongest in the meta and which ones might need some attention. Tier lists are frequently updated after patches, as balance changes (nerfs and buffs) can shift the strength of different Brawlers. Here's an overview of the current **meta** (as of January 2025) and where certain Brawlers stand.

S-Tier (Top-Tier Brawlers)

These Brawlers dominate the current meta due to their versatility, strength, or game-changing abilities.

1. **Emz** - Great range, consistent damage, and utility with her super. Can be effective in almost any mode.
2. **Stu** - Fast, high damage output, and great mobility make him a threat in all modes, especially **Brawl Ball**.
3. **Leon** - High mobility and stealth make him a top pick for **Showdown** and **Gem Grab**.
4. **Mandy** - Huge range and burst damage that can control zones effectively.

A-Tier (Strong Brawlers)

These Brawlers are strong but may have a slightly less universal presence or require specific strategies to be highly effective.

1. **Shelly** - Still a powerhouse in close combat, especially after a recent buff.
2. **Brock** - A great long-range damage dealer with explosive abilities, effective in **Heist** and **Brawl Ball**.
3. **Carl** - Balanced and reliable, with good damage, control, and versatility.
4. **Max** - A great support Brawler who excels in speed and mobility, great for teamwork.

B-Tier (Solid Brawlers)

These Brawlers are generally well-rounded, but they may not be as overpowered in the current meta. They can still shine with the right strategy or team composition.

1. **Nita** - While solid, her damage output can be inconsistent in higher-level play.

2. **Darryl** - Solid tank with good mobility, though he struggles against long-range damage dealers.
3. **Poco** - As a support Brawler, he can heal his teammates but needs strong synergy for maximum effectiveness.
4. **Barley** - Great for area control and slowing down enemies but requires careful positioning.

C-Tier (Situational Brawlers)

These Brawlers are less common in the competitive scene but can be effective in specific modes or under specific circumstances.

1. **Rico** - Fun and versatile, but often lacks the damage output or survivability of higher-tier Brawlers.
2. **Tara** - Good for crowd control, but often too squishy to stay alive in higher-stakes matches.
3. **Colette** - Powerful against tanks but struggles against ranged or evasive Brawlers.

Note: Always consider the current patch when using tier lists as balance changes could shift the tier placement. Experiment with different Brawlers based on your playstyle and the mode you're playing!

Cheat Sheets: Quick Reference for Maps and Counters

Having a quick reference for **maps** and **counters** can help you make smarter decisions when you're in a match. Here's a concise **cheat sheet** for Brawl Stars that covers common maps, key Brawler counters, and some general tips.

Popular Maps and Recommended Brawlers

1. **Gem Grab**:
   - **Best Brawlers**: **Leon**, **Emz**, **Max**, **Stu**, **Poco** (Support)
   - **Avoid Brawlers**: **Darryl** (may struggle to control the middle)
2. **Showdown** (Solo/Duo):

- Best Brawlers: Leon, Shelly, Nita, Carl, Brock
- Avoid Brawlers: Poco, Tara (relying on teammates can hurt in solo)

3. **Heist**:
   - Best Brawlers: Brock, Barley, Max, Stu, Tara
   - Avoid Brawlers: Tanks (unless they can really dominate or control an area)

4. **Brawl Ball**:
   - Best Brawlers: Stu, Max, Leon, Darryl, Nita
   - Avoid Brawlers: Poco (unless healing is a major factor)

5. **Knockout**:
   - Best Brawlers: Emz, Brock, Leon, Carl, Nita
   - Avoid Brawlers: Squishy Brawlers like Poco or Tara

Brawler Counters Cheat Sheet

- **Tanks (e.g., Frank, Darryl, Bull)**

- o **Counters**: **Brock**, **Barley**, **Bibi**, **Sprout** (long-range and crowd control)
- **Long-range Brawlers (e.g., Brock, Penny, Piper)**
  - o **Counters**: **Darryl**, **Shelly**, **Tara**, **Stu** (close-range and mobility)
- **High Mobility Brawlers (e.g., Leon, Stu, Max)**
  - o **Counters**: **Emz**, **Penny**, **Barley**, **Sprout** (area control)
- **Support Brawlers (e.g., Poco, Pam, Nita)**
  - o **Counters**: **Leon**, **Penny**, **Brock**, **Barley** (high damage)

Pro Tips: Insights from Top Players and Streamers

1. **Adapt to the Meta Quickly:**
   - o **Pro Players**: Top players know how to quickly adapt to balance changes and update patches. Follow streamers and watch tournaments to learn

which Brawlers are dominating and adjust your strategies accordingly.

2. **Focus on Map Control:**
   - ○ **Pro Tip**: In **Gem Grab** and **Heist**, controlling the **center** of the map is often the key to victory. Always prioritize map control and avoid wandering too far from the objective. Use Brawlers with area control abilities like **Barley** or **Sprout** to keep enemies at bay.

3. **Use Gadgets and Star Powers Smartly:**
   - ○ **Pro Players**: Top-level players know when and where to use gadgets and star powers. Don't waste them—time your abilities to create huge advantages in clutch moments. For example, **Max's Super** should be used when your team is about to engage in a fight to boost your movement speed.

4. **Team Synergy is Key:**
   - ○ **Pro Tip**: When choosing your Brawlers, think about how your

team's composition will complement each other. A combination of **support**, **damage**, and **tank** can make all the difference in competitive modes. Learn to synergize with teammates—especially in modes like **Brawl Ball**.

5. **Use Positioning to Your Advantage:**
   - **Pro Players**: Top players are experts at positioning. If you're a ranged Brawler like **Brock**, position yourself behind obstacles or in areas with good visibility of the map. Don't expose yourself to unnecessary damage, especially in **Showdown**.

6. **Adapt Your Strategy in Showdown:**
   - **Pro Tip**: In **Solo Showdown**, avoid being overly aggressive early on, and focus on gathering **cubes** without drawing attention. In **Duo Showdown**, working with your partner to ambush other teams is often more effective than going for solo eliminations.

7. **Watch Tournaments for Strategy Insights:**
   - ○ **Pro Players**: By watching **Brawl Stars** tournaments or competitive streams, you can see how top-tier players handle different Brawlers, maps, and modes. They often share tactics or decision-making strategies that can be crucial to your improvement.

Conclusion:

By utilizing **tier lists**, **cheat sheets**, and **pro tips**, you can gain a significant advantage in **Brawl Stars**. Keep yourself informed about the current meta and adapt quickly to new updates, modes, and Brawlers. Test different strategies, prioritize team synergy, and always look for ways to optimize your gameplay based on insights from top players. By staying updated and continuously learning, you can become a more skilled and competitive player in the game!

Chapter 10. Conclusion

Brawl Stars is a dynamic, engaging game that offers endless opportunities for growth, learning, and fun. As you work your way through the ranks, experimenting with different Brawlers, modes, and strategies, it's important to reflect on the progress you've made and celebrate the milestones along the way.

Celebrating Progress and Achievements

1. **Track Your Achievements**: Whether it's unlocking your favorite Brawler, reaching a new **Trophy Road** milestone, or winning a **Brawl Ball** match with friends, these moments represent your dedication and skill. **Brawl Stars** rewards progress, so take pride in the small victories—each

achievement contributes to your overall success.

2. **Special Events and Tournaments**: Participating in special events or community tournaments adds another layer of excitement to the game. Even if you don't win every event, these experiences allow you to grow and learn from top players, boosting both your skill level and enjoyment.

3. **Improvement is Key**: Every game you play is an opportunity to improve. Don't get discouraged by losses; instead, use them to analyze your gameplay, adjust strategies, and try new approaches. You're not just leveling up your Brawlers, you're also leveling up as a player.

Encouragement to Keep Practicing and Enjoying the Game

1. **Keep Practicing**: The key to becoming a master at **Brawl Stars** is practice. Even if

you've already climbed the Trophy Road or unlocked all your Brawlers, there's always room to grow. Each game is a chance to refine your skills, whether it's improving your **aiming**, **movement**, or teamwork.

2. **Enjoy the Journey**: Brawl Stars is designed to be a fun and rewarding game, and the best way to experience it is to enjoy the journey. Explore different game modes, test out new strategies, and immerse yourself in the evolving world of **Brawl Stars**. It's not just about winning, but having fun and growing as a player.

3. **Connect with Others**: **Brawl Stars** offers a fantastic social aspect with **clubs**, **friends**, and online communities. Share your wins, learn from others, and join in on the camaraderie that makes this game even more enjoyable. Whether you're playing solo or teaming up with friends, the connections you make enhance the experience.

4. **Stay Curious**: The meta is constantly shifting, new Brawlers are introduced, and special events keep the game fresh. Stay

curious, experiment with different strategies, and embrace each update as an opportunity to learn something new.

Final Thought:

As you continue your **Brawl Stars** journey, remember that the most important thing is to have fun and enjoy the game. Whether you're climbing the Trophy Road, mastering new Brawlers, or just hanging out with friends in a **Club**, there's always something to keep you engaged and entertained. Keep practicing, stay positive, and most of all, enjoy the game—there's always something new just around the corner!

Happy Brawling!

Printed in Great Britain
by Amazon